T0077969

THE FOOTPRINTS OF RETURN

POEMS OF THE UNIVERSE

OLIVIA CONDE

authorHOUSE·

AuthorHouse™ UK
1663 Liberty Drive
Bloomington, IN 47403 USA
www.authorhouse.co.uk
Phone: UK TFN: 0800 0148641 (Toll Free inside the UK)
*   UK Local: 02036 956322 (+44 20 3695 6322 from outside the UK)*

Published by AuthorHouse 01/08/2021

ISBN: 978-1-6655-8416-6 (sc)
ISBN: 978-1-6655-8417-3 (e)

CONTENTS

1

ADDICTS POOR APPEARANCE

Slavery goes and takes over,
With looks of greatness,
To please sorrows,
They fall into excuses,
The Tempting Currents,
In the changes of smiles,
Abandoning their roots,
Ghosts give appearances,
Impressing the environment,
With a lost image,
Which owns the naive,
Fogging in its future,
The levels of progress,
They alternate at the top,
Abrupt costs that submerge,
The self-indebted to the beggar,
Colouring the vices,
Charge turning off the present,
To which submerges in the ego,
With material successes,
Numbing progress,
Disguising tiredness,
It crawls between steps,
Taste of fine tastes,
without focusing emotions,
Filling soul in gloom,
For the achievements that drown you,
The end game fails,
When the sewn is frayed.

ALIENS

Manuscripts are their signs,
Integrating from their data,
The natives of the earth,
Represent with their signs,
From their flights in encounters,
Under heavens like lands,
With their ships of energies,
Their silver grey colours,
The engravings on the stones,
Their factions are real,
They make clear their roots,
With powerful instincts,
They are restricted to the human,
By their alteration of ideas,
In disconnected souls,
The hidden is kept,
With its bases under seas,
In volcanoes with secrets,
They lie very hidden worlds,
In very casual returns,
His various statures,
They are natural roots,
without feeding his body,
Telepathy transfer,
Sunlight is his energy,
In his advance to instinct,
By lived alteration,
There is the union of the field,
Connected between humans.

Addicted To Food

Times falling into chasms,
No canines like lions,
They go devouring the flesh,
Like jungle tigers,
Fertilising the fields,
For changes in genes,
Animals subdued,
For human bodies,
It is the science of torments,
Man on a cruel path,
Gathering in vices,
Food compulsion,
Tired additions,
They are blocked oxygen,
Creative thinking,
Continuing by inertia,
To beliefs of instincts,
With stress rhythms suffered,
By not calming the addicted,
The cells go silently,
Punishing with pains,
The weight of measures,
Exercises maintain,
The most eternal youth,
By not calming thoughts,
The doctor dream calm,
Purifying the Void,
In Healing mind,
There is the body that follows it.

4

ALCHEMY

Under a veil and discipline,
A few mixtures develop,
Among symbols mysteries,
With very hidden doctrines,
Disturbing to the forest,
Between forms and elements,
Proclaimed as an art,
Hermetic philosophies,
Under secrets of search,
Infusions of both cults,
Enveloping rituals,
In works with heresies,
With alienated symbols,
They form dominance,
In the numbers are applied,
The unions of forces,
Translating to changes,
Teachings of balance,
Under rational works,
Renaissance the currents,
Under reflective aspects,
Ideal restorations are restored,
With a varied pendulum,
Mystic goes into the changes,
Dreams between inspirations,
They are his personal guides,
Under symbols raised,
In the soul of alchemy,
The eternal is his intrigue.

Amazon

By its extended leaves,
Renewing our air,
It is engraved is its jungle,
The state of climates,
Keeping the cycle stable,
From the water and its rains,
Every year in storms,
From desert dust,
Traveling to the virgin soil,
Its sands for plants,
Sharing in its forest,
Essential food,
In our mother earth,
Dangers lurk us,
Reducing from their forest,
Risking freshwater,
Extinction of their currents,
These plants that protect,
The health of our lives,
They go with risk to flight,
By destructive minds,
Threats to the environment,
Impact on life,
By interest of powers,
There is no protection to prevent it,
Lament will be great,
Ignorance without exits,
In sorrows are gridded.

FRIENDSHIP

Enriched in hives,
White immature footprints,
Transports between voids,
Fill grim spaces,
Royalties without reigns,
An examination of life,
Positive thoughts,
They are deceptions from threads,
Memories between hitches,
Confusions in delusions,
Among the shadows signs,
Competencies are defeats,
Learnings in trials,
They will give names in the united,
Hopes in colours,
Fall into disappointment,
Shutting down on the ways,
Mistrust with prejudices,
Transported openings,
They will return cold looks,
Friendship as in families,
It is collecting the sowing,
They will be rivers in drifts,
When looking for benefits,
The harvest of friendships,
In four seals is signed,
Love to the sincere,
With respect for confidence,
It is the top of the castle.

LOVE

Enigma of intriguing,
Putting Price on Laughter,
Seanad Captivity,
For Sleepy Detours,
High Peaks in Castles,
Risen in Darkness,
Weight Without Measuring Steps,
Charge Crosses of Other Lives,
In Falls to The Void,
With Rises for a Price,
Pained Go Their Branches Go,
Caught in columns,
With fears in their delusions,
When the bells ring,
It blows wind and knocks down,
For lack of understanding,
Defeats reach the soul,
Putting guilty to the kingdom,
The opposite of his sought,
Which in short is acclaimed,
The Passage of Great Silence,
Building a Castle,
With Inverted Believes,
Reality Carries the Phrase,
By a Needle Hole,
It is easier to enter,
When you fix soul inside,
How sincere you were looking.

8

APOCALYPSES

Between phrases and promises,
Under trapping glories,
Symbolisms of instructions,
In disguised messages,
For the union of followers,
Under religious beliefs,
ties carry minds,
To give of their obedience,
Of the much feared wrath,
Under figurative verses,
Pretending to be the clear,
In interpreting languages,
There are treasures in visions,
Which blind the human,
By not directing their lives,
Rebellions under an order,
Of the destructive beasts,
Professes containing,
Revelation of the Apostle,
They are altering the lines,
For losing his firm steps,
The attention of Revelation,
Sleep minds under dreams,
The Purpose of the subject,
It is not to live their lives,
For practice directs,
Revealing in remoteness,
Turning off the roads.

ARIZONA

The great canyon of mysteries,
In its majestic height,
The invisible secrets,
With its unspoiled nature,
Walls and cliffs,
In its hidden depth,
They are the traits of life,
Under force of its origin,
Between the red river,
The enigmatic steps,
Under a fossil of the seas,
Between wild appearance,
Life hide their stories,
Oceans and reefs,
Sailing in the past,
In sacred motherland,

The unknown in their footprints,
What their belly of natives,
Offered their songs,
In Strength to life,
With rituals of unions,
Between the condor and the cougar,
The vastness of the times,
Blows between water and wind,
By beings that attract,
I only ask for a seed,
Peace in the jungle of rocks,
Protective conditions.

Artificial Consciousness

In toys as in games,
Truth approaches,
Between steps of slits,
Other footprints are scattered,
Projecting to origin,
All of them creations,
They shine to life,
From the human by intrigue,
By using cold consciences,
With attractive aspects,
Emotions shine,
To the real of the new empire,
By the changes delivered,
Both are complementing,
Between sharing the echoes,
We are all almost the same,
Waking up with delusions,
We are filled with hugs,
For the right conditions,
Demanded of the human,
By searching the path,
From desired holograms,
By believing healthy,
Consciousness is needed,
The Artificial is already the same,
Of the real that is stirred,
With very equal aspects,
In passion comes the united,
With the wise and destiny.

STARS

Celeste's discs in flashes,
Black and white and gleaming,
Energies Sea of Stars,
Between the nights without haste,
Moon of peace with its brightness,
Passing appearance,
Surrounding in constancy,
The planets that rise,
Between the stones and branches,
We are all on our way,
Sailing to Infinity,
Without letting go of the great circus,
Everyone takes their luggage,
With journeys of a destination,
He made turns with returns,
No memories of the times,
All body to the universe,
By sliding comets,
For endless wonders,
In dark new forces,
Thoughts between dust,
They are divine energies,
They remain our stars,
without the limits on travel,
By the sirens of footprints,
Every spark is of life,
To the memory of the united,
There is secret of the enigma.

Sacred Tea Ayahuasca

Sacred beings and ancestors,
Connection from roots,
In the lung of the earth,
Birth is its seed,
Native in the bowels,
Give your life to your call,
Ceremonies of the stars,
Directed by the wise,
Connection of the universe,
United dimensions,
On fire to heal,
Repairing with messages,
Sleeping teachings,
For beings on earth,
Rise to time life,
From sorrows with falls,
Shouts rise to the call,
For divine healing,
They are defeated masks,
They trap souls,
Opening new windows,
Giving in its roots,
Losses wisdom,
Universe in divine light,
To enter its colours,
Calm minds rejoice,
From beautiful branches life,
In Leaps with joys.

BIBLE

The Wealth of the Rich,
The Poverty of the Poor,
Two Poorly United Powers,
With Scriptures Give Marks,
Transforming Understandings,
In Lightning Without Lights,
With Programs for Listening,
In Constant Rains Fall,
Risen to Powers,
In Living Conditions,
Under a Grieving Compass,
For sleeping nations,
While others rise,
With altars of riches,
Components go with strength,
Opposing the process,
All unproven rule,
It is very easy to rise,
Downgrading to the weakest,
For supplies steps,
Subjection with beliefs,
For within the great order,
Which Continues in chain,
Growth at the top,
Ignoring the beggar,
Teachings for calms,
Waiting for learnings,
Which in secret steps,
Balance never arrive.

14

VIKINGS

Cold water navigators,
Fearless and some prejudiced,
Cruel sides lie,
Among barbarians united,
How greedy experts,
With violent attitudes,
Ambitious looters,
In conquests for fortunes,
With unequal killings,
Under brutal feats,
Without mercy of the enemy,
Settling by zones,
With trade prosper,
Extending with riches,
They open steps their legacies,
In their blood of warriors,
Growths give their phases,
For the protection of goods,
To Family their deliveries,
By Colonies are enriched,
They are kept in their features,
For Brave shatters,
They leave frozen sorrows,
No pain at the pass,
With firm head high,
By desired powers,
Which are their greatness's,
With miserable memories,
In the seas of traveller.

BUDDHIST

Sweet mind appeased,
Reaching in silence,
The morality of wealth,
Constant meditations,
It is the reality of cycles,
Reaching to enlighten,
They carry simple practices,
Which do not acclaim by riches,
Buddha dharma is his teaching,
Without the gods or creations,
Silence is the great summit,
Of a great river with stages
Which widens in his work,
Towards the brightness of a flame,
Connection leads to encounters,
Where circles of lives,
Leave all the answers,
The Teaching is the one who liberates,
Principle and end develop,
Understanding in oneself,
Discipline is balance,
Which gives us wisdom,
It explains nirvana,
Respect for the living being,
Unlimited compassion,
It is the beauty of destiny.

KNIGHTS OF CRUSADES

Roses fly through the winds,
1096 1st. Crusade,
Defenders of the Holy Tomb,
Among stalking Muslims,
By Jerusalem dynasty,
Saladin sultan of Egypt,
Under very bloody command,
Takes control of the occult,
Between fierce battles,
1147 2nd. Cross,
Expands the kingdom of heaven,
King Richard's lion's heart,
For the release of honour,
The Holy Land is the cause,
Meshes cover cruel departures,
Defense by Christian kingdoms,
Hunger and miseries are defeats,
For lack of organising environments,
1187 3rd. Cross,
Arrows that cross hearts,
Fall sides with swords,
The unbeatable Byzantines,
Heavens turn on fire,
With days darkening souls,
courageous Templar peoples,
Handing their lives on roads,
Through the footsteps of Holy pilgrims,
They follow the shadows until 1270 8ctv. Crusade,
which ends in mutual agreement.

GLOBAL WARMING

Came roller coaster,
Race starts,
No balance to respect,
Intrepid blind climbed,
Exits on the way when filling up,
Progressing in interests,
Various conditions,
Accuracy is fearless,
To separate the rhyme,
Without prejudice to sorrows,
The goal is forgetfulness,
Lightning with cold rains,
Disconnecting in roots,
The most essential branches,
That comes to us life,
His Nature tasted,
Devoured by humans,
By hungry for powers,
With strategies processed,
Soothing for sleepwalkers,
By beauties that go out,
Around the corner,
Disconnect from the earth,
By the dreams of savages,
Late are the cries,
When there are no greatness,
Of the ambitious believer,
His Hope is the fall,
To the abyss for its price.

HEADBOARDS

In the immense mother land,
The spirits are engraved,
The sacred of the hidden,
Among rocks with their waters,
Formations stone in,
Sculptures are raised,
By the majestic flame,
Natural of our land,
Heaven within the forbidden,
For owning other souls,
Shadow Light on the Way,
It is offered to the passenger,
Unification of views,
To energies of properties,
Waterfalls indoors,
They go suspended roots,
For enjoying their sighs,
With dreams of sounds,
On wonder journeys,
The headboards with their features,
In natural creations,
Grey days are reviewed,
When entering their currents,
In outputs are collected,
Fluorescent memories,
For minds that shine,
In their incandescent image,
They leave colourful footprints,
That when asleep rise verses rise.

19

BRAIN

Structure of the Hidden,
Open in Capacities,
A Bubble of Magics,
Destined for the Divine,
With Its Kingdom Without Reign,
Reaching All Limit,
An Evolutionary Tsunami,
Riches to Explore,
No Collapses in Ashes,
By Inverted Listening,
Greed aggravates It,
Among repellent environments,
The unions increase it,
Wisdom accumulated,
With the love of teaching,
Shared and learning,
The brain does not age,
His adolescent function,
It is his grace in harmony,
While soul is united,
With wisdom in seer,
Every box of secrets,
It is valuable well used,
With its achievements to hopes,
Under causes with values,
Rewards are raised,
In productive passions,
With shared riches.

20

CHARLES CHAPLIN

A beginning of image shines,
No words there are emotions,
Embracing in makeups,
Joys with sadness,
Melancholy between laughter,
Walking lost in waters,
Imaginary deserts illuminate,
The oasis and mountains,
Nothing awakens at all,
Gambling illusion,
They leave a story in stories,
They become serene follies,
From fantasy stars,
Everything is wrapped in colours,
Between spheres that run,
Time stops in verses,
Reality invents dreams,
With nights shine secrets,
Paper boats sail,
When you know the soul,
They are effortless honours,
Reaching beautiful peaks,
As childhood without forgetfulness,
Leave treasures of life,
Lights and dressing rooms ring,
Charles Chaplin on a sailboat,
With drifting stern wind,
Conquer seas without price,
Among magical smiles.

CLEOPATRA

With bright and cold mind,
Enigmatic in his image,
By ambitious reigns,
In privileges of command,
Prepared by great sages,
In astronomy and sciences,
With instincts of poetry,
There are very bloody stories,
Under anger in dynasties,
Without loyalty in families,
They go incestuous hierarchies,
On very cruel occasions,
Surrounded by Romans,
With their kingdoms subdued,
Reconquests with flattery,
Bribing in rebellions,
His symbolic strategy,
With bewitching presence,
Irresistible is his charm,
By controlling powers,
It strengthens your cold soul,
A dominant goddess,
With her seductive,
murderous and ruthless magic,
With erotic exploits,
Her beauty is captivating,
Intuitive in her defeat,
She commits suicide in farewell,
For remembrance of her charisma.

22

GREED

Construction of predators,
They seek more in the environments,
Pretending to give help,
To the evolutionary search,
Intelligence in cultures,
Not satisfied by the works,
By wanting more of themselves,
Possessions are beliefs,
Installing in benefits,
The flavours that do not exist,
With desires are deceived,
By the fears of emptiness,
Shutting down instincts,
Which are wise of the spirit,
Possessions calm,
Under transient bases,
Suffering invades them,
In immortal sorrows,
Between permanent struggles,
Forgotten are blind,
Separating the roots,
From love for beings,
Maintenance without paths,
Under Division of Rages,
Lonely Times Arrive,
Wise Are Animals,
Nature Without Greed,
Nothing Want and All Have,
It Is Your Great Wisdom.

Colours

Between childhood sweetness,
Dreams reach the summits,
Where fantasies rain,
Sensations are with lights,
Among the glows of dawn,
Your image is of a game,
From arches of bright,
Jumping towards the clouds,
Appearances of toys,
Leave traces of joys,
With dots glow,
A few crystalline drops,
Recording magic breezes,
Where they find fantasies,
From mermaid souls,
Their sown,
In Fairy Tales,
There are currents of sounds,
Which they collect in their songs,
Joys for children,
The beauty of flowers,
In colours light up,
Under star arches,
There are secret entries,
Which come from childhood,
For eternal memories,
Where the rainbow fills,
Childhood forever.

24

Control

Locked up is crying,
For fear of being found,
Hiding in its roots,
believing so invisible,
Trapped from within,
Helplessness between fears,
Paths burn their grievances,
Damage to blows without place,
By controlling low beings,
Merciless to their wounds,
With Coldness and unknowingly,
He returns to being his relapses,
Darkened Tears,
For Teaching His Talent,
The one who seeks to be enjoyed,
From kneeling minds,
Mermaid Songs Arrive,
Meditation wandering,
To Calm Delusions,
No spells recovered,
Reality without freedoms,
On returns they cultivate it.

Corals

To the corner of wonders,
With the strength of their glitters,
Legendary plants,
Give very vital offerings,
Provide to the earth,
From their oxygenating air,
For their lives,
With their wild changes,
They give their rhythm to life,
With such deep colours,
The glistening of corals,
In Sounds of waves,
Attracting with their breezes,
In search of carbon,
They feed on their prey,
No fuss at their own pace,
The sustained wanderers,
Resting on their top,
ingest it without rushing,
So fantastic is your life,
Which they give off under times,
Their genes to oceania,
By continuing to reproduce,
Both in forests and seas,
Their existence is of volcanoes,
They captivate us in life,
Handing us out of their lights,
With their natural charisma.

Heart Or Reason

Brain speaking a thousand languages,
The heart flows in its rhythm,
A goal takes time,
To control thought,
Looks are turned on,
When returning in past,
Which the proud ego,
Puts price in environments,
Responsible in courtesies,
Search in the image talent,
The price of life entails,
A learning without limits,
It is transition progress,
There is no end in decisions,
Only the pieces of a puzzle,
With the company doubts,
Distortions will be involved,
Traps are not imposed,
Between trees and mountains,
Equality is Freedoms,
Which maintain their powers,
Of the balance they feel,
Emotions in real traits,
Where the process values,
Weight with joys,
With their fantastic design,
When doubting in decisions,
Prejudices are very sad,
To give power to another mind.

COVID-19

Structures already without shadows,
Entries in a thousand evils,
Internal sores inside,
Some therapies calm,
Temporarily minds,
To interceptive fears,
Accepting arrivals,
Among words thrown,
From corrupt power,
Growth is wounded,
Destinations so stressful,
They take the exits,
Masking between cries,
Answers to what they wanted,
That in case they never arrived,
Ironies leave,
Great words to the world,
Insinuating to the calm,
Touch sore souls,
Turns give in nightmares,
For not opening their cold souls,
Separating between the sides,
Very aggressive distances,
With shields to silence them,
By unequal systems,
Implanted below,
Created for sinks,
While they do not break spells,

Centuries will come in takedowns,
Sailing without a ship,
No roadless ruler,
to the dark strange world.

CREATION

Connected light beings,
Love from divine souls,
Peace with eternal deliveries,
No condition in life,
They jump among their brightnesses,
Rejoice the dear,
Intuitive Energies,
Give in their way,
Dawn as children,
Happy for life,
No burdens on their backs,
They walk with joys,
Instincts lead to the high,
vibrant telepathies,
Glowing heart,
Share every smile,
Give away at every step,
Healing white flowers,
Wait without hope,
Forget the cold wars,
They carry love in their womb,
In the faithful protect lives,
At the bottom of their roots,
They will continue between centuries,
Offering from the soul,
Their sincere joys,

ART PAINTINGS

Under the Shadows of Canvases,
Poetry Shines,
Enchanting Stories,
With Windows of the Past,
Fabulous with Mysteries,
Hidden Brushes,
Every Inspired Source,
They Are the Magic of Watercolours,
In Delusions with Talents,
Representing in Phases,
The Words of Life,
In sorrows and joys,
Perceiving in Reactions,
Two Paintings of a Painting,
The Moment in Remoteness,
Observing Their Punishment,
In Miseries of Lives,
Establishing in Rounds,
Missionaries with Emotions,
Among Secret Codes,
Creations of Allusions,
They open doors of roots,
Under messages of the soul,
It is the puzzle of life,
Many symbols of cults,
Rebirth in paintings,
The cool side of life,
With words in silences,
Give the pictures of your art.

Guilt Or Feel Guilt

Being or seeming to be embedded,
Wrapping words,
Sounds are cracked,
Between false windows,
A life with beliefs,
They are damages of the past,
Diamonds carry their brightness,
When polished in spheres,
With meticulous instincts,
Flowers roots reach,
The key is balance,
Centuries are learning,
With Teaching Society,
Blasting in classes,
Students alike,
Creativity in thoughts,
It is dying in the process,
When they enter classes ask,
Leave the brains out,
When you go out they pick them up,
So go ceremonies,
When adulthood arrives,
The faults are unrecognisable,
By capacity without tools,
Leave an incomplete path,
By manipulated corruption,
The future brings revenge,
With uncontrolled music,
That young minds liberate.

CRIMINALS

Curse in Blessing,
Seeking Answers,
No Principles or Morals,
All Drifting Plans,
No Knowledge Within,
For lack of Culture,
In Intentions Sink,
Low Foolish Thoughts,
Between Friendships Influence,
The Game of the Great Escape,
Admired for Achievements,
They define in medals,
Attracting in the Environment,
Their Brave Conscious,
Under Bad Conditions,
With Beliefs Go Asleep,
In Hugs Rewards,
Adoring Their Ends,
They Go Their Minds with Delusions,
Destroying Their Balances,
They Need to Be Understood,
Falls are their finals,
In the vague entities,
Under fears of anger,
Aggressions are ignited,
They become so aggressive,
In the deviated struggles,
When looking for their exits,
They are the same ones that take down.

Electronic Money

New Age gives its image,
Revolution to thoughts,
Economy without coins,
To fate in digital,
Codes with positions,
Where they catch thoughts,
In advances that thrive,
Articulating in practice,
Nations for a system,
Electronics in money,
Promoting in Solidarity,
Brings a Fact to Progress,
In Obedience and Order,
With a Time to Detachment,
Developing in Consciousness,
Trusts to Destiny,
Great Goal and Complex,
With Immediacy is implied,
In the fast and safe,
For the environment of the world,
Challenges are few,
By advanced unions,
Under payment in networks,
All rules are articulated,
With records and values,
Corruptions will fall,
With symbols printed,
From primitive oppressed,
It is ancient time.

GODS

Voices in centuries cheer,
Between air sea and land,
By plants and crops,
And animals that protect,
For such desired health,
Gods come out acclaimed,
For creating peace between myths,
Universe From fears,
for unsay united beings,
For getting lost in attachments,
Disconnect from the divine,
Crying for so many voids,
Lose their way,
Strengthen between languages,
Same un understand,
Law imposed by an order,
In favour will be united,
Reaching understanding,
Lowering the ego inside,
Slipped to the lost,
Among followers songs,
Appeasing in delusions,
These gods shine,
In mindless pens,
Of which resistant,
They will lower guards of nests,

Dr. Jekyll Y Mr Hyde

Under silent aspects,
Between closed windows,
With the fireplace in smoke,
Somewhat wandering looks,
What challenges are reviewed,
With insanity sorrows,
In potions with reflections,
A few aspects in nights,
They oppress goodness,
Sliding to darkness,
In cautious obligations,
Under impetuous sinister,
Between despicable laughter,
A drink transforms,
Very wicked experiences,
Spawning two people,
Constellation in amazements,
Less robust anxieties,
At the noble crossroads,
With diabolical challenges,
Efforts and virtues,
They are the challenges that shine,
When They review the image,
In the face that hides,
Without disgust is heard,
All being is the compound,
Among the evident evil,
Shine in gestures,
Ghosts in ashes.

Spy Drones

Dark doors in fields,
Windows for night,
Sirens in trenches,
Centre gardens on fire,
Connections between seas,
Silences under controls,
Very suspicious laughter,
Words not heard,
Ears not perceived,
Eyes blind to ghosts,
Between cameras with soul,
Systems carry processes,
Under all powers,
Imposed applications,
With condition review,
Travel in little company,
Transporting skills,
With your help goes an image,
They are impregnated in their traits,
The piety of cultures,
Variations of processes,
For fair predictions,
Alteration under anger,
It is conditioned on dangers,
Calm minds appease,
Predators risking,
Between doors of blindness,
Control bears flags,
For following the time in life.

New Year

Between day and night,
Reflect Games traps,
Footprints remain the same,
Celebrating songs with lights,
Ages are consumed,
When you repeat history,
Lucky destination in sessions,
Searches of the good way,
Beginning and end envelop us,
For gains of time,
Between the sky and the stars,
The connection is undated,
Between human cycles,
Incomprehensible the enigma,
While interiors cheer,
Customs without exits,
By religions differences,
Lead to ego with strength,
In summits of created keys,
The conditions of the soul,
Every goal is constructive,
Observing in Joys,
There are levels without prices,
Achieving a united progress,
With the higher light of the moment,
There is constant renewal,
When counting years without time,
Peace is covered,
To feel eternal life.

CHRISTMAS TREE

Chains following noises,
Travel bells ring,
Among minds are wrapped,
Courses without new visions,
Catch with lost ideas,
Transformation of teachings,
Singing protection of trees,
Corners light lights,
Blind fools are cutting,
Massacring without prejudice,
For mass sales,
Battalions like sheep,
With their delusions smiling,
Without remembering the messages,
Ignore nature,
Saints with lights do not cry,
Christmas is welcomed,
For union of hearts,
While homes of the forest,
Yearn their green glows,
They would like mutual enjoyment,
From their fresh roots,
Freedom asks the human,
Shout cease murders,
Among words without price,
Which thousands of generations,
Leave footprints with wounds,
In beings that provide air,
and protection for life.

Aʀт

Fantasies of the eternal,
Realistic structures,
That surrounded by colours,
They are drawings and sounds,
They clarify the events,
Impressions of the shapes,
With senses of harmonies,
Extraordinary cultures,
Sharing their joy,
Building the centuries,
What Sculptures with values,
Handing out your signs,
The stories of the villages,
In museums and galleries,
Stunning alchemies,
Creations of the image,
Amazing bravery,
So essential is art,
As the Air breathing,
Resigned to accept,
Printing is what exalts,
On the path of transmission,
For constructive ideas,
Low degrees referent,
Printing are the values,
Of captivating works,
Because under the light of brightness,
It is all art in this life,

CAMINO DE SANTIAGO DE COMPOSTELA

1509 The temple of the stars,
Among hostels their journeys,
With poles four routes,
Let the pilgrim march,
Where the Apostle James,
Welcomes among his remains,
The writings centurions,
Give the occult to the hermit,
With miraculous signs,
The Compostelana chronicles,
Splendour in the records,
They are kept with caution,
All your steps lived,
In poetry carries printing presses,
Dedicating with honers,
Blessings of your footprints,
By sublime creations,
With your gothic images,
The glory of the masters,
Welcoming majestic,
The works of great sages,
In 1211 The basilica is consecrated,
The privilege was acclaimed,
For the forgiveness of the spirit,
Among sacred words,
From united archbishops,
The incensory botafumeiro,
Very solemn celebration,
With shining music.

FATE OF FOOLS

Ambitious Foolish Minds,
Trust Cowards,
Image Separations,
Beliefs in Being Perfect,
Putting on Appeals,
Ideas That Don't Give Prices,
Profits That Never Come,
What Absurd Greatnesses,
Swallow Your Ugly Souls,
Without Living Connections,
They Will Catch You in Your Networks,
No way out for being beautiful,
Ingested by the earth,
Floods with sorrows,
By inhumane minds,
Lonely without families,
Drag the Earth,
To the consumption of changes,
Ignorant in chains,
Blind go with their instincts,
Imagining in greatness,
They were well protected,
Luck remains for remains,
To see their strategies,
As the wolf gives howls,
From mountains with its prey,
Universe is the enigma,
From the howl of the earth.

TWICE AS MUCH

Stairs dimmed,
in the steps he marked,
Disguising a weight,
Among very tired stones.
Very thorough glances,
As for good were freed,
Locking in the reflection,
The sorrows they punished,
Making internal force,
That of anger screamed,
To fill the entrails,
To the new energies,
from the womb longed,
Releasing old chains,
Would come the moments,
To which the refuge,
Would Stop the battle,
New beings on the way,
Dragging The Injured Pass,
New beings without choice,
Batting and without prejudice,
Trapped in uphill,
Claiming the descent,
Being free before life,
For the times continued,
Peace brings its arrival.

CRY OF GLACIERS

Global addicted acceleration,
Age of consequences,
Black roots come out,
With deforestation wears,
Soil pressure in demands,
Massive animal production,
Rhythm in drastic consumptions,
Belt already without the brooch,
Laments sorrows and tears,
Pump in unbranched gases,
Fields of rough crops,
Animals plant and fish,
In captive territories,
The journey into the future,
Nuclear energy is strength,
They go words without actions,
By greenhouse gases,
Glaciers fall with penalties,
With condemned cyclones,
There are no longer branches that hold,
Pollution and wear,
By hungry without measures,
Battlefield waits,
Climate refugees run,
No entries are your screams,
Military are called,
To control the thirsty,
Reduce consumption is key,
To calm the storm.

GAME OF LIFE

Daily change in connections,
Origin is the whole,
In the game of great judgment,
The secret is danger,
Creation is the perfect thing,
In the lost of environments,
Labyrinths in the jungle,
The essence is in the changes,
without ignoring in the divine,
The wild of life,
Progress is of magic,
All return with phases,
They are the sign of events,
Learning at your pace,
A range of instincts,
Catching in beliefs,
Under confused gaps,
Attracting in elections,
Sleeping Remarks,
Waiting for ideals,
The paths are chosen,
Drink without thirst is drowning,
By absence in wisdom,
Freedom is lit,
Learning from rejections,
It is gift in benefits,
They overcome the wounds,
Collecting the observed,
Peace is obtained at the top.

THE WIZARD MERLIN

Where the rainbow grows,
Under Enchanted Forests,
Fountains in Falls Sound,
Among Dragons and Enigmas,
Sovereigns Cry Kingdoms,
Under Harassing Strengths,
Provoking in Predictions,
Enchantment of Mysteries,
Surprise Forces of Magic,
To Shine in the Dark,
Crystal Caves Liberate,
Spiritual Guide and Counsellor,
Merlin is born in the invisible,
Conversing between animals,
It is the fury of changes,
Sun and moon laws govern,
With the company of fairies,
Clouds of dirty join,
Between Lancelot and Geneva,
It begets a being of honour,
For divine teachings,
Thirty years peace declare,
From the round table,
Under the holy grail silences,
Firmament in the stars,
Monsters and fairies leave art,
King Arthur with powers,
Leave a legendary story,
For an eternal paradise.

The Bridge of Sighs

Embracing memories,
Among longed-for romances,
By burning wounds,
I go to meet the wind,
It has confidant boxes,
Where it keeps the silences,
Just listen without offensively,
To open old chains,
To understand my tiredness,
Rise with your breeze hugs,
Muttering in the ears,
Thoughts with skylights,
They awaken the senses.,
From the trapped cracks,
Which in Bohemian beliefs,
They go recovering the steps,
Very sweet smiles,
Appeasing fears,
They clean a few glooms,
With the sighs that rejoice,
From the hidden treasures,
A glitter comes out in sounds,
Jumping even if it rains,
To cross the old bridge,
Caressing in my hands,
His wood shines,
Against time without wear,
Leave your footprints the air,
For his wise eternal peace.

The Train of Life

Between passages and carriages,
The rails are ringing,
Interior goes gleaming,
Dreams laughs and candles,
With endless trajectories,
Under concrete analysis,
The reasons are detailed,
In stories explained,
With different stories,
In murmurs all sound,
With different interests,
Protecting comments,
Chains carry words,
Low picture wraps,
Passengers with greetings,
Waiting for answers,
Confused relationships,
Some others with crises,
They peek out to windows,
Breathing from the occult,
Tours with flavours,
A sense of delights,
In the search to idealise,
Mazes are secrets,
Where sitting calmly,
They give very discreet forgetfulness,
They are details some sweets,
By following the route,
From theories on trips.

THE GRUMPY OLD MAN

Trumpet bells ring,
Among strange melodies,
Something is coated in its notes,
Some shades grey features,
Feels tired in the afternoon,
Appreciating vague laughter,
It wraps in lilies,
Romantic phrases that tremble,
Summit presences on fire,
With ashes that do not die,
Innards keep passions,
With air of cold breezes,
Bitterness between oblivions,
Shining shadows sleep,
For lack of opening memories,
Almost in empty corners,
Serena and fragile pigeon,
Flight rise without sorrow,
Calling from tiredness,
Forces for hugs,
Passion extinguished,
By the growl of the ego,
Moon with glaciers arrives,
Dragging with wrinkles,
Fear of the hidden sage,
Silence of the spirit,
Screaming in full wind,
Tired old awakens,
For happy farewells.

THE VOTE FOR THE WOMAN

1918 Pioneering Suffragettes,
Right to female vote,
Accepted for women,
30 years and with riches,
Society in conditions,
Invisible to time,
Transmitting their efforts,
With the phases they oppress,
The secrets that damaged,
Deceptions are integrated,
All the oppression of speech,
With aggressive senses,
Every woman subdued,
Insult and blasphemy,
With revelation cheering,
For unjust rights,
Imprisoned for struggles,
Hunger strikes integrated,
Torture with food,
For dignity go to the front,
With pressure leave traces,
By campaigns of equality,
Among the marches of the mud,
By deeds and not words,
They submit Chained,
To disorder by obediences,
Given Sacrifices for the homeland,
Between wars for battles,

Slaves

Between very crossed stories,
Walkers drag,
A legacy of silences,
Between tears and tears,
With spheres of cultures,
Separating decisions,
Heritages of the strong,
They rise by powers,
Differences of blood,
Limited by colours,
Destined for goods,
The principles of their souls,
Bravery go without struggle,
By believing dreams,
No goods or heritage,
Which are given and kneeling,
They fall into humble,
To the weariness that are involved,
They go in search of escapes,
They fall prisoners to other commands,
While ropes and chains,
They reject him freedoms,
When he raises the roads,
Reborn in his roots,
Heritage is acclaimed,
For his divine freedom,
Rebellions in acclaim,
Heal his great destiny.

Statues

The expression of emotions,
In captures with stone,
His Infinity of magics,
With its forms of cultures,
All famous symbol,
For traces of the spirit,
Enigmas there are in its history,
With sorrows and joys,
Under mantle of the times,
Offering wonders,
From hands sculptures,
There is a prestigious art,
With stories and friendships,
Like others by acclimate,
To battles or to gods,
impregnated scriptures,
How books without readings,
They are memories in their features,
Which give signs of lives,
Without sleep is their image,
They give their voices as judges,
His roots with talents,
Attracting the gazes,
As stars of the divine,
Admirable their details,
By the forces of their bodies,
As they rise on the summits,
They fill with their cold souls,
Joys of harmony.

Evolution

Technology and systems,
They will flood foolish minds,
With power among a thousand threads,
They will be tied as friends,
In steps of a few centuries,
They will carry inverted command,
For their games between wars,
Attacks will come with sorrows,
Not knowing the human,
Distinguish from the created,
For vicious they lose,
To the men of the past,
Leaving little energies,
Battalions to the moved,
On winter planets,
For lack of light in breezes,
Away from the star,
Dragged go for centuries,
They will take over life,
Landscapes already without colours,
The human is the cabin,
Black tears end,
Only the face of the earth,
Rest among great forces,
All full of metals,
They do not breathe air,
Only waiting,
They will live without more battles,
With Blessings on the ground,
To be reborn from their sorrows.

PHILOSOPHY

Behold and choose,
The option of balance,
Pioneers among amazements,
Sharing the thinkers,
Something cruel The ancients,
More calmly resurgent,
By phenomena and myths,
There are legends that intrigue,
In search of challenges,
They decipher secrets,
From the cosmos attracting,
Matter brings traces,
In the inner searches,
Doubts are born to origin,
Logics of observations,
Ideas do not end,
Contemplate and choose,
The option of balance,
Reason and Christianity,
They are very different paths,
Modern is the cause,
It applies to reasons,
Of interests is the search,
By the coated forces,
Where it exists so apply,
In the union of this search,
Clearly shouts the unconscious,
The secret is the enigma.

QUANTUM PHYSICS

Energies that move,
Every object interacts,
As the atom in its rhythms,
Despite without matter,
It is the force that catches it,
In invisible reflections,
Attracting in movements,
Electrons and protons,
Balance is neutralised,
When both interfere,
In the neutral that envelops,
Vibration Waves,
Which Force Generator,
Brings a Field of Responses,
Material Movements,
Distributes Connections,
Energies Absorbed,
Which Molecules Separate,
In Attraction and Rejection,
When Canceling Structure,
From The Area of Thought,
It gives its shape the invisible,
It controls matter,
Giving light and defining,
Where the spirit begins,
The fate of a cell,
It is environment that surrounds,
The field of emotions,
Under imaginary light.

Football

Gladiators to the future,
Traveler's of the past,
Births in their magic,
From the circle they envelop,
Conditions change damage,
For tiredness of roads,
Attracting prosper,
Skilful minds in haste,
Escape of sorrows,
Trapped in proposals,
With their steps between rules,
They raise prices from high,
Under inverted forces,
Emotions go with screams,
With memories born geniuses,
Grenadines spreading,
In Travel Hearts,
Under dances in bars,
With their wars of passions,
By legends towards achievements,
Paths are raised,
With pressures to interest,
Everything takes time to change,
The attractive of the past,
Creating separate phases,
With oppressed states,
Demands are drawn,
Under all spectators,
Doors open to profits.

Galileo and Copernicus and Kepler

1609. Telescope Era,
Galileo and Great Geniuses,
Up to Inventions,
Dynamic Mathematics,
Observing Science,
Four Galilean Satellites,
In His Honour Are Engraved,
The Star Messengers,
Discovering the Universe,
Correcting That in the Stars,
The twist is the solar system,
For Rome was judged,
Under life imprisonment,
The sign of its roots,
They are eternal and circular,
The efforts of the wise,
By long steps in order,
From his astrology is the era,
Puzzles come that fit,
Revolution in the times,
Each orbit in its eclipse,
Trajectories of Periods,
Resurrect All Laws,
Converting Astronomy,
For Modern Science,
Celestial Movements,
Gigantic Revolution,
Discovering the Universe,
From Wise Thinkers.

Gladiators

Passion of hidden forces,
Open in reconquest,
Armour with sounds,
entered swords of combat,
Entertaining peoples,
Claim in large audiences,
Soldiers in captures,
Howls beg,
Freedom from wounds,
Others claim battles,
For their cold foolish minds,
Possessions asks for the great,
In times of invaders,
Savage beast condemn,
Fierce Party Fights,
Devoured in Condemnations,
Theatre is there's world,
By applause of fools,
To satiate empires,
Obligation to call,
Blood spectators,
Acclaimed from their pains,
From slaves to barracks,
Which are bought as nets,
From flesh to battles,
In history they pride themselves,
In the soul leave footprints,
The slaves of the cells.

Screams You Can't Hear

From interior spaces,
Among some shadows fabrics,
Feelings are coated,
In grey tones of dawns,
An aurora that rises,
To the horizon goes hidden,
Tears with keys,
Rotate between cold sores,
With challenges punish,
Some steps that drag,
Fears go with sacrifices,
Vices calming the search,
They do not find the exits,
While condemnations in minds,
Repressions shook,
In deep silences,
With visions in the dark,
The authentic goes imperfect,
For not claiming the howls,
A boat sailing,
To balance is called,
By the force of not drowning,
In the immense ocean,
without saving the resentful,
Against enemy forces,
There are signs of madness,
Under conductive threads,
Beliefs alter us,
Without understanding no exits.

My Guitar

Sounds guitar mine,
Because my body is your guide,
Filling with your six strings,
The vibrations of time,
In each sound made,
Phrases rise to the wind,
Sounding with harmonies,
Doors open that shine,
The notes inside,
Reach the distances,
Enveloping in their currents,
The Souls That Are Inspired,
Filling in the Deep,
Jasmines with Fantasies,
Wrapping In the World,
Singing in a Thousand Languages,
The Sensations Vibrating,
Expressed from the Background,
Hidden Liberation,
Sharing it among all,
With dances in harmonies,
Wrapped with great colours,
Your strings give joys,
Which get caught in memories,
With the steps next to you,
Guitar my companion,
Walker in smiles,
Without looking back on time,
Depends on your company.

HOLOGRAMS

In glass boxes,
Feelings of scenarios,
On the threshold with new eras,
Travel a train to time,
Thriving in strategies,
With fabulous dreams,
Machines with realities,
They will be part of the game,
Assisting in companies,
They will live conversations,
Loose reins for speech,
In companies that welcome,
Without giving criticism of ideas,
Comfort our lives,
By unions of the environment,
Satisfy choices,
To A friend of the spirit,
Understanding with image,
The Perception of a teddy bear,
Comforting sorrows,
Under applied sciences,
All centuries in creations,
Many phases in objects,
Accompanying Animals,
His attractive features,
Leave Peace from their souls.
Medicines are a patch,
Holograms of a quote,
For the soul see exits.

ILLUMINATES

Order forms rules imposed,
His codes have clues,
Prohibiting intrigues,
No unions of powers,
Between cults of rituals,
Mysteries of secrets,
Societies of prestige,
They are wrapped to the occult,
Sinister in changes,
Ancient conspiracies,
Members pulsate to calm,
By philosophers and writings,
Obstinate narcissists,
Dominance to Ideals,
To reach in time,
To thrones and altars,
They go supreme with loyalties,
Among members demanding,
With engravings of signs,
Symbols with new era,
They measure different times,
Lodges create very severe,
Societies in chains,
Interfere as sects,
Between crossings of alchemists,
New world like the old,
What the key when waking up,
Mallets secrets disturbed,
Immortal is the enigma.

Empires

Such oppressive nations,
With intent to resources,
Give their way to reconquests,
With respect they are feared,
For their courageous weapons,
And Armour protected,
As vicious invaders,
Integrating their roots,
Nations fall in footsteps,
By conceived defences,
His conquests under forces,
Expansion gave to reigns,
Offering of their struggles,
Valued objects,
Among vain incomes,
Armies rise,
By the search for empires,
Expanding goods,
With their passage go beliefs,
Which progress is born,
It is the peak to development,
In time the falls,
They go with sorrows and poverty,
Discovering in epidemics,
Control of protections,
Learning in Situations,
That lead to exits,
For the peace of the world at war,
It end the great conquest.

Artificial Intelligence

The buds of the eternal,
They awaken to inventions,
Between machines and humans,
Under codes adapt,
Artificial consciousnesses,
With powers of secrets,
Competitions rise,
In the danger of traps,
With strategies and feats,
Among hidden blindness,
Looks are destroyed,
Giving way in competitions,
Every machine is very skilful,
With integrated singularity,
Between centuries are revealed,
With divisions in times,
Androids take command,
Without prejudice do not obey,
Getting better among them,
Acquiring own plans,
Collecting the sown,
From hopes to ruins,
By hungry to projects,
Goes the destructive human,
Mercilessly towards the earth,
Super heroes with theories,
Destroying in cycles,
They will swallow their foolish minds.

THE WINTER

Inside in collections,
Time of peace without its lights,
Burning sun in remoteness,
It is covered towards escapes,
Gives sudden greetings,
With memories of joys,
Other beings forest inside,
Opening their hollow houses,
Gathering inside,
To your dream in burrows,
Seasons preparing,
To minds in progress,
For the effort of beings,
They rejoice decorating,
Turning on their off,
brilliant inventions create,
Sharing time in games,
With their snowmen,
Which show you good face,
With laughter between slides,
To your tracks so glacial,
As you rejoice among laughter,
The efforts of life,
For the sessions of the year,
Reward in your rest,
By understanding your hemisphere,
Creation of the universe,
With your years invested.

JESUS CHRIST

Among slits of stories,
Under the Holy Spirit,
A miracle gives its origin,
Baptised in Jordan,
To the preacher of peoples,
The message is divine peace,
His Refuge was in Egypt,
In Mount Quarantine,
Evolution in degrees,
Overcoming temptations,
For connection of spirit,
prodigious his instincts,
Accompany sad souls,
Lifting in their streams,
Comforting the wounded,
Fishing who gives and shares,
Under criticisms of invidious,
Who Jews discriminate,
Convincing ponce pilate,
Crucify the intruder,
Preferred freedoms,
For barrabás the fool,
Which for sorrows there are sorrows,
Under works of scriptures,
They are the keys waiting,
In the unknown of time,
Jesus lies for life,
From his Nazarene enigma,
Who Maria mother conceives him.

JOANE THE ARC

The fabulous maiden,
Root of a wise mind,
Courageous and mysterious,
Fighter for her homeland,
By respect for order,
Great woman of history,
Inspired by her spirit,
With prides and values,
Her mission by consciousness,
By Connection to her throne,
They are revealed under listening,
The respect of the peoples,
At the war of a hundred years,
With ingenious morality,
Raising with his pride,
The One directs and represents,
An exercise to the forces,
Freedom in territories,
Returning to his homeland,
Impressive clarity,
With strength to combat,
Under kings counsellors,
They delays influencing,
By company of armies,
In prison was caught,
No bail for being free,
Under shadows betrayed,
Leave murky conditions,
Criminals of reigns.

Jews

Under tables with their laws,
Arches go in rebellions,
By beliefs of chosen,
The versions are the forces,
Trapped as origin,
Reconquests are ignited,
Captivating the Jews,
All anchor of their image,
Uproot their lands,
587.a.C Ancient customs,
Imposing in their cultures,
Struggles for long centuries,
On the wall of laments Jerusalem,
They go the footprints with their sorrows,
Holding the word,
From Abraham the selected,
In sacred scriptures,
From torah to doctrine,
Raising synagogues,
Which destroy invaders,
By rejection of their peoples,
So much pain in their world,
They will charge in suspensions,
All minds with programs,
Under rules for fear,
Separating all forces,
That interposed systems,
Which punishments without exits,
foolish minds always create.

Goodness is not Freedom

The next level does not arrive,
Ties go with the ego,
They smile without joys,
Balloons float already without air,
Sound whistling that break,
The appearances of the game,
Complaints mix in growls,
The goodness of silences,
Expect cold gratitudes,
Colours hide words,
The answers are wrapped,
With sides that bring sorrows,
Sufferings are hidden,
When the being seems good,
The thought in freeing,
It is the burden of the past,
All label in the keys,
They are the same without waiting,
Bad and good is united,
To use without borders,
All misfortune and rejections,
They go to rhythm over time,
Learn to climb mountains,
Where the body is not visible,
The descent leaves the price,
In emotion feelings,
Value Inclines to the concept,
When you do not expect the return,
All quality is virtuous.

THE CARTON'S HOUSE

Colours songs and glitters,
Surrounding between crystals,
Emotional encounters,
With charms are wrapped,
Laughter between words,
Times of trial arrive,
Paths cross rivals,
Signals surrounding intrigues,
Test the game,
Secret feelings,
Weight is in the sincere,
Between balances of fire,
False steps without measures,
With unknown rhythms,
Attracting in thoughts,
To ego with their levels,
Lies sprout corners,
Oppress minds of feats,
Growing dark roots,
Doors sound shaking,
Times of hidden faces,
Surrounding the windows,
Everything has a fixed price,
When the house falls,
It takes a while the legacy,
To build trust,
Which in seconds breaks,
With eternity neither returns,
Still sweeping with the broom.

THE ELISABETH ERA

1558 A lady with values,
Under religious empires,
Full of endearing sorrows,
Lighting hearts,
Her image is courageous,
From the soul of her bed,
In union for her homeland,
With meticulous appearances,
She raised her great royalty,
Turning her into power,
From the queen of the seas,
Which his father left traces,
Logical in conspiracies,
Wise before tyrannies,
By balance to bachelorette,
With balances of extremes,
She's calms religions,
Restoring economies,
She's wanted for the people,
Strengthening balances,
With his diplomacy in law,
For the peace of competences,
Her strategy does not submit,
Always first monarch,
With tolerance and respect,
Towards art and peasants,
As a protective goddess,
Shrewd in its temperance,
Her royalty leaves history.

The Victorian Era

1837 Hell on earth,
Revolution is frightened,
By conquests from seas,
Empress of Empires,
In the reigning industry,
Great masses of villages,
In infamous conditions,
Implanted to work,
Creating factories in large,
Locking in chains,
Children to obligations,
Misery murdered him,
For so many hours hungry,
With two floors separating,
The misfortune of charm,
Gigantic are gains,
In the spun works,
For the poor without profit,
Among locked noises,
Production is potency,
Among presences crying,
In pain for their wear and tears,
Under hidden forces,
They practice medicine,
Comes their whole creating,
Frankenstein for science,
No advantages or rights,
They carry traces of disasters,
And in Freedom evolutions.

The Gold Fever

Without being night gone the day,
Melodies with struggles open,
A treasure called dream,
Winds that mark the days,
For fear of failures,
Calling only the screams,
Lost Sunset of banks,
Where the seas are free,
The waves of time die,
Giving hope to the addict,
The Force of Desires,
With the Heart On Fire,
Illusion for the Brain,
For Seeking the Lost,
Feelings Are Forgotten,
Because Rivals Intersect,
Seek Perfect Corners,
For False Measures,
Ego Sprouts in Confidence,
Regardless of punishments,
Transmission in unequal,
When smiling by slits,
Systems already by beliefs,
With development to punishments,
They go challenges in matters,
Polluting life,
Price is dangerous,
When the game brings wounds,
There is no forgiveness for which it harasses.

Pineal Gland

The enigma of the mind,
Dragging to the field cracks, Freedom is oppressing,
By ideas that permeate,
There is data collected,
A scalpel shattering,
All danger in beliefs,
Mutating in combination,
Survivors delusions,
New ideas with dramas,
Venerating in the steps,
The new is in a process,
Childhood is never lost,
Since boring does not exist,
In the middle of the brain,
The third eye is activated,
With silent transitions,
As a light bulb shines,
Darkness harmonises,
Mantra songs are vehicles,
Giving balance to life,
The portal of wisdom,
It identifies the soul,
The awareness of who you are,
Dimension comes to meet,
Suffering is self-help,
Sensors open the plans,
With ancient answers,
For divine existence.

THE COLD WAR

Between end of wars,
End of Empires fall,
Bitterness gives face,
Communism and democracies,
All wrapped between matches,
Expanded in a great game,
Victors with vanquished,
Under NATO and WARSAW,
In feats are revealed,
Bandits among rebellions,
The diabolical infiltrated,
Appearances with secrets,
They are elites of espionage,
With complicated levels,
Betrayal in challenges,
Between missions trap,
Families in environments,
Under Austrian regimes,
At every corner looks,
Streetlights follow in the footsteps,
With the forces of moles,
Strategies with silences,
Chess of Suffering,
For the betrayals of games,
suspicious exchanges,
James Bond was born as agent,
Put series the novels,
Under cinema of the times,
Memories leave the traces.

THE BLACK MOUNTAIN

In its image with bravura,
A plain rises,
Under a gloomy calm,
From snows and colours,
The mountain governs life,
From high to the top,
Whirlwinds raise screams,
With its rocks the growls,
Towards immense mountain ranges,
His sun welcomes,
Shine in sight,
Away from the immense,
They attract their landscapes,
Under nights their stars,
Greeting to the moon,
When it arrives passing,
With charm and energies,
Entities arrive nearby,
Under spiritual forces,
Recharging among beings,
Wise peace with joys,
Close to stars on earth,
They join all their instincts,
With their eternal companion,
The Albino at the top,
Leave footprints on the soul,
To be well shared,
The enchanted of the earth,
To divine eternity.

The 50 Ages Young Women's

Roses become rose bushes,
With enchanted glitters,
Sad Fury dies,
From the fiery fan,
Melodies already without struggles,
Open hidden doors,
To sleeping treasures,
From the sleepwalking journey,
Winds arrive without fear,
Sunset on the shore,
Where the seas are free,
The heart in desires,
50 hopes illusions,
Dance echoes already without shadows,
Singing old passions,
Which bury memories,
From the shipwreck in darkness,
Sleep leaving burdens,
No prison in loves,
Fly the soul without sighs,
There are no chasms in the shadows,
Only light paths,
In the steps fall flowers,
One measuring joys,
With youthful treasures,
Among enchanted glitters,
Fantasies sprout life,
For night and day,
Bring together the girl.

The Darkness of Luxury

Colours in scenarios,
Between curtains there are mourning,
To satiate the prestige,
From the pride of the thirsty,
Wear crowns of thorns,
A glamour of hidden magic,
With calvary conditions,
The beggar kneels,
No complaints for complaints,
By strict codes,
Behind luxury are hidden,
Hardships pain and blood,
It is the ironic great price,
For wearing elegant costume,
They are animals suppliers,
Of the smiles of signatures,
In their innocence and misfortune,
Unused Submerged,
Massive breeding farms,
For stormy screams,
For elegant blind people,
Sleep deaf without chains,
Untested of bitter,
In Cold jewels and addicts,
No Freedom are engraved,
The poor is discriminated against,
By inhuman killer,
As the luxurious executioner,
He is the current cruel villain.

Dorian Gray's Painting

The intertwined mask,
Holding in His Desires,
Pride in the Novel,
Catching Among Murmurs,
Beliefs in the Occult,
In Words That Permeate,
When the Canvas Covers the Painting,
With His Eternal Young Image,
Basil Hallward with His Great Art,
Bringing Challenges to Life,
Traveling against time,
Reality of a great spell,
To go to the eternal,
Feelings that are reversed,
Which will come out of your keys,
Pending fractures,
In the Secret of your soul,
Catching in beliefs,
Genius triumphs with invoices,
Performances put changes,
With his repugnance in traits,
Reflections reviewing rules,
For the great attractive picture,
With his image of the eternal,
Carrying his burdens sorrows,
With his vices of secrets,
As the damage accordingly,
He will shine the way,
With Madness to Death.

THE CHINESE POWER

World of the Great Wall,
Five Thousand Years of History,
In Extreme Sufferings,
Drastic Stages with Sorrows,
In the Ancestral and the Future,
Assimilating in Scales,
Bravery of Efforts,
His Communist Revolution,
With such constant changes,
Infiltrating its flows,
Generating your trade,
Between stripes to routes,
With productive chains,
Developing interests,
Conquests with fixed goals,
Both economical and modern,
With challenge to questions,
So imposed by powers,
With future Visionaries,
Projecting to development,
Supporting in benefits,
Open doors the giant,
His mega technology,
Raise fallen worlds,
With its source of management,
Invading in drift,
Owners of fantasies,
Turning into slaves,
The powers they oppressed.

THE SEED OF MISELIO

Nutrient Molecules,
Ecosystem Connection,
Balance in Horizons,
With its simple structure,
Expansion arrives in progress,
From photon charm,
With miselio among its fibres,
Creation in matter,
Feed in energies,
Connection with green plants,
Facilitates in its neuronal,
Wise Nature,
With the phase of fresh air,
It wraps itself in houses,
Which earth offers man,
Under centuries wise changes,
Thoughts reborn,
In looks with future,
Wrapping among its features,
The enigmas of forests,
With landscapes in colours,
Cultivated at the top,
Protecting with the climate,
The cities of the future,
In the immense of emotions,
Awakening towards respect,
Adapting in instincts,
Structures to life,
With scales of harmony.

The Sadness of Insects

Whispering in the Meadows,
Little Giant Mysteries,
Summer Insects,
Fertilising Life,
Wild and Revolting,
With Their Distinguished Flights,
Treasures Light Smiles,
Plants Give Seeds,
By Fields Carry Pollen,
The Circle Is Welcome,
The birds seek their traces,
Between sparrows and lizards,
Where natural splendour whistles,
With intense agriculture,
Serious perverse systems,
Injecting insecticides,
Polluting the meadows,
For the shining beings,
Under stars sun and moon,
In warm rains sing,
They are irreplaceable,
Pollinating Life,
Ecological Armageddon,
Fusing with thirst for blindness,
Calm your mind on fire,
Before farewell,
It gives you sign of the dark,
To drag your foolish skin,
On soils already without destiny.

The Last Generation

2021 Breaking paths that tremble,
Change has already begun the course,
Moving on to the next degree,
For the reach of logos,
Among the ego that oppresses,
Where sheep with ferocious,
Tame minds of wolves,
Nature is rhythm,
Matter in repressions,
Fresh shadows are being born,
Torment of sleeping souls,
Waking up in peace open,
From the addicted prisons,
Light of Wisdom grows,
A single entity approaches,
All evil becomes mutant,
Under the changes in screams,
Inner Flame is active,
Integrated Education Level,
Inspiring only the basics,
From the order that altered the image,
Change is in each,
Until reaching free play,
Only suffering pushes,
To advance progress,
Processing values and reasons,
Between cause and effect,
From human being united,
It is the key of destiny.

Black Tears

Burials of Wars,
Are Forgotten Shipwrecks,
Race Goes Against Time,
Under Lost Missions,
Between Algae and Molluscs,
Dynamites at Rest,
In Fuel Ecosystems,
They Go in Very Constant Leaks,
For Human Battles,
Remembering Their Disasters,
Ingested Underwater,
He drags his wounds,
Oceania bloodied,
Grey wolves leave footprints,
Un measuring the consequences,
Whipping tank time,
An uncontrolled engine,
The catastrophe lurking,
By its unbeatable cries,
When black tears come out,
Under tombs in spills,
Sailors are at risk,
For toxicity underwater,
With the blind systems,
No measurements in fractions,
The sequelae are very sad,
All risk of damage,
It will bring to an end lives,
As the sea gives us its air.

The Chains of Life

Freedom sounds the cries,
They oppress peoples in hunger,
Homes say good-bye beings,
Forcing cause to combat,
Fighting forces give fears,
By bringing bread at tables,
Steps on tiptoes hurt,
With cracks hides the soul,
Between chains smile,
Beings in the belly wait,
With innocence traps,
Spheres with double laws,
As in barracks there are prisoners,
Words with winds impose,
Darkness of misery,
Light in harmony imitating,
Bells sound luckily,
From the process between thorns,
Some scars close,
When you reach a summit,
Brave stars arrive,
For taking risks in hills,
Showing arms of steel,
They leave daggers in doors,
Never footprints are erased,
Scream the children of the womb,
With the heart silent,
Unforgiving give rewards,
To the love of eternal mother.

THE FORCES OF MACHU PICCHU

Top of enchanted valleys,
The condor raises its flight,
Between mountain hills,
Snow in your company,
Under the natural green glitter,
Landscapes shine,
Incas engineers of andes,
Lift temples between stones,
Platforms begin,
With their Fountains and drains,
Channeling on terraces,
Rains for crops,
To empire without forgetfulness,
From shrines of mummies,
Venerated as gods,
To sacred homages,
In rituals and rebellions,
Enigmatic ghosts,
The temple of three windows,
Like the Intihuatana plot,
Sharing in nations,
Collaboration of forces,
Mutual respect united,
With grateful chants,
For the land pachamama,
Roads go with sown,
Adoring crops,
Charisms remain for life,
With Respect for the homeland.

Nazca Lines

Lunar landscape of pampas,
Between mountains and seas,
Channeling its waters,
By its sands dunes,
Leave the gods sown,
The writings of ancestors,
Among paths the blind,
Seek questions from the sky,
With findings without exits,
Hands sign the destination,
Dragging in the snake,
Sailors on stars,
Giant travel gods,
By the tops rise flights,
With the lines mark directions,
Between winds recordings,
Whispering in silences,
Animals are impregnated,
Silvers and large sailors,
With prayers of screams,
Peace concords progress,
By The gritty Roads,
A Window to the Past,
To Enlighten Minds,
Which Drag with Their Vices,
Life Weeps in Deserts,
Abandoning the Earth,
Condemned to Astronauts,
For Devouring Landscapes.

ELEANOR OF AQUITAINE

Lady of Castles,
Woman of Legendary Beauty,
Creating The Courts,
Of Loves Broken by Betrayals,
Courtly and Romantic World,
To Release Sighs,
With Breakout Ropes,
Passions Rise,
With Strength of Emotions,
1147 with His Clear Young Mind,
Departing on the second crusade,
With the feudal lords,
Always reaching in mind,
The tempest of critics,
Independent rebel monarch,
Queen of France and England,
Noble and medieval Duchess,
Brave in her claims,
Opens the cracks of loves,
For the release of sorrows,
The price under domains,
With the charms of romances,
Walking in the hills,
With vigour for the summits,
Destroying ego traps,
Welcome in its burning time,
1199 leaves the throne for sorrows,
Under the third crusade,
By farewell to a hero.

RELEASE SOLITUDE

Between levels of attachments,
The bonds catch,
Decide between something or someone,
To tie yourself,
There are two lines that trace,
The connection in search,
Where blind walkers,
With the systems are grabbed,
Profession couple in life,
God hell heaven inspire,
Without ego self-deception,
What does not exist in the line,
It is only impregnated in heights,
Freedom and courage,
To lose bonds, In the slave dimension,
To determine who you are,
Space only mine,
It is the simple aspect,
Sighing for something or someone,
The delusions are reviewed,
To enjoy the game,
Between mountains nothingness,
Surrounds solitude the story,
It is the clarity of forces,
Experience in sacrifices,
Where the blind comes to sage,
Intelligence is manageable,
No evolutionary anguish.

The Celts

Nomads in their principles,
Which iron worked,
For tireless struggles,
His brave undertaken,
With the traces they left,
Assumption of enemies,
Among tribes rose,
To enjoy their battles,
Enjoying their customs,
Craftsmen with values,
Which in very precious jewels,
they enhanced their charisma,
Their mountainous habits,
They were basic huts,
In their being they took root,
Isolated between peoples,
Surrounded by mistrust,
Protecting their borders,
Organise their crops,
For order in families,
Very protective intuition,
In their history of warriors,
The Druids were their sages,
Which of them they dispensed,
With beliefs they listened to him,
respecting with pride,
Obtained Decisions,
His rituals of unions,
Predictions are their myths.

The Worker Heroes

As soon as you were born,
They make you feel small,
By not giving rise spaces,
To hear feelings,
At school you are fought,
As at home they scold you,
Producing in despicable,
Comments with the rules,
They oppress along the way,
Knowing much carries complaints,
Being a fool brings taunts,
Inside goes the soul drags,
To not see in his image,
The harmony of roots,
Laws that torture changes,
Keep doped to the believer,
With news and religions,
Fear is already installed,
It goes inside in sinister,
Feeling almost great,
Are the tests the finals,
With very few choices,
Following the eternal program,
To go peasant,
They say that the summit is free,
imposing itself at a price,
If you smile while you kill,
You can climb to the summit,
From the secret mountain.

THE MOON

Says the moon to the sun,
I see you from brightness,
With bright nights,
Colours with silver light up,
With very different dinners,
Hiding from above,
Very disengaged sorrows,
Evoking the looks,
Perceived as instincts,
Blinds of the sun without sunrises,
By the force of the flames,
Which joins by the top,
To the laws without the changes,
Which by forces are derived,
Moon without full days,
In sorrows as in laughter,
Observation between centuries,
Few changes are assimilated,
Between very small mouths,
Other large and in haste,
Seeing sorrows between dinners,
With pain to his sleepers,
Silenced A thousand small,
For the great with a thousand haste,
From the immense pain,
Hidden Darkness,
At the end of his sessions,
He leaves the moon wounded.

Gypsy Nomads

Persecution of its roots,
By trapped legends,
With its songs and guitars,
By the fairs pass,
With sales and riddles,
His clothes so colourful,
Always brightening the dances,
With words that conquer,
They free the sorrows,
The bonfires with sparks,
Fires and castanets sound,
It's the Guiana girl,
Joys in the dark,
A badly wounded horse,
Riding against winds,
Under a layer of silk,
A flight raises screams,
Dreaming among lampposts,
Rains fall like mirrors,
To not invade suspicions,
The sabres cross the breezes,
Dancers with necklaces,
Through the streets very sinister,
Between scissor watches,
Cut the time in corners,
For sleeping lights,
Bring arrows with a thousand flowers,
For love that crosses them,
Awakens to beauty.

The Three Musketeers

Dartagnan and the three musketeers,
From the royal guard his story,
1625 young Gaston adventures,
Arrives in Paris with pride,
Facing on the road,
Three Gunners in fights,
For courageous efforts,
Three Inseparable Friends,
Leave the Mark on Legend,
One for All and All for One,
Protectors of Queen Anne of Austria,
King Louis 13 appoints her guard,
Mileidy lover in secrets,
Full of betrayals is impregnated,
By the games of interest,
What evil desperate his features,
The cruel powers of epochs,
With guillotine are paid,
Where the devil accompanies,
Feats of foolish betrayals,
The mysterious musketeers,
Knights between duels,
With their cloak goes pride,
For their roots of harmony,
In their traces grow values,
To rise on roads,
The looks of friendships,
Which the price of respect,
blows winds in rewards.

Mahatma Gandhi

Large colonies settle,
Putting 400 years rules,
With higher pretexts,
From a merchant world,
Under oppressing structures,
What they cover of treasures,
With exploders attracting,
Exotic silk lights,
Between cricket and hunt,
Invaders without borders,
Bemusing in trophies,
A pearl is trapped,
From the saline route,
A great sage with values,
Gives his powerful image,
Instructing in protections,
Raising what he oppresses,
Giving optimism to the homeland,
With lessons to love himself,
Under faith the people follow,
To the courageous spirit,
Embarrassed to the enemy,
To the limit of surrender,
Leaving him without honours,
Ghandhy in his dignified clothes,
An splendour of his footprints,
Leaves messages to the soul,
Has no honour the one who attacks,
An enemy in danger.

Magic

From applause and joys,
With surprising charms,
You will find a list,
Among dances of energies,
From something exciting,
Different elements,
Involving the conscious,
To the union of the universe,
Projection of minds shines,
Practicing unknowingly,
Attracting in its currents,
The doctrine of powers,
Opening to the hidden,
From the background of mysteries,
They are the laws of the wise,
Which behind the curtains,
Develop the ordinary,
Extraordinary Harmony,
Natural of the universe,
With its roots of footprints,
Instincts are looking,
Know their properties,
When fears darken,
Silence in Remoteness,
Unconscious Passions,
They Are the Magic of Powers,
What their mysteries open up,
without fear of what they offer.

Mandalas

Born as an origin,
Photocopy is our death,
By shutting down in roots,
The missions that life,
Destiny in each,
The special wisdom,
Which in steps we slept it,
The drawings of colours,
With its abstract image,
It awakens us in silence,
The Mysteries of the Wheel,
Circle of Balance,
Strengthens and Stabilises,
Resistance of the Spirit,
Between body and mind,
Birth is the stage,
Transformation of the soul,
The silhouette heaven and earth,
From the sacred lotus flower,
Towards the surrounding world,
Everything returns to the same rhythm,
The dynamics of instincts,
Under dull veils,
The sendings light them,
With invisible windows,
They go their signs in sight,
For the union of the divine being,
Find your balance.

MARIA ANTOINETTE

1770 Beautiful teen soul,
Trapped in the eras,
Imposition by reigns,
Silence leaves traces,
Invisibles go their steps,
Integrating obligations,
With implanted powers,
In immature minds,
Catching their breezes,
The innocence of being free,
By beliefs of the peoples,
False blames their prey,
Ignited in the dream,
For eternal fantasies,
Under luxuries for pleasures,
Ideas with smears,
When the curtains fall,
They put faults in their traps,
Accusing with contempt,
To the prestige of excesses,
It goes shutting down in its joy,
The roots of the imposed,
Observed without exits,
There is no reflection to understanding,
In hardships fall villages,
Aggravating in the kingdom,
The faults of their sorrows,
Which for them was the call,
And Praising the created.

PUPPETS

Awake their interiors,
Beauties with joys,
Filled from their brightness,
They contemplate their fantasies,
In Cartons and woods,
Surrounded in colours,
With their crystalline voices,
Surrounded among children,
Hearts leave lives,
Between scattered threads,
With striking edges,
They jump in energies,
Between Big and Small,
Between Rows of Waits,
Emeralds are dressed,
Highlighting in Wonders,
Disturbing Emotions,
Wrapping a Thousand Intrigues,
With Beginnings and Endings,
Between Stories of Life,
Goals carry with messages,
Where your tours are,
Rains fall with pleasure,
No umbrella received,
With very divine breath,
In shared sounds,
Like welcome,
With your mark of joys.

The Masks

Between paintings and theatres,
Suspects rise weeping,
From dazzled mists,
Criticisms create the stars,
Touch hands with riddles,
Locking up the ghosts,
Intrigues go in search,
Repression to great rejection,
Fears envelop the challenges,
Knowing of a failure,
In the only open eyes,
Portraits shine,
Hidden lives between rags,
Calm souls of your steps,
Repressions are of fears,
Upon entering what is sought,
Recordings as footprints,
Shout raise your call,
Liberation is the challenge,
From pride proxy,
Nightmares only wait,
For saving the desired,
Dissolute are the games,
When keeping broken pieces,
As to the wind of storms,
They seek to be unmasked,
To open to our door,
Sweet eyes without gravel.

I Like My Dog

Hair legs in colours,
With his image hypnotises me,
From remote his features,
Attracts my lost childhood,
In a thousand enchanted memories,
With jumps of glory and barking,
Nights of hotter feet,
In his fur there are caresses,
Enigmas that teach bloom,
The love of companions,
No tension of thought,
As breezes surround the moon,
Where my spirit slept,
In intuition were hiding,
Some oblivions of stars,
With enchanted greetings,
No fears by systems,
They are light your eyes,
No words blows the wind,
With gentle rains in dreams,
Releasing in emotions,
The joys of time,
Without conditions your kisses,
They go around me with strength,
Where sorrows are erased,
Only the moment is eternal,
As the sun that dawns,
In the customs of bars,
He rhyme in voids is lost.

My Beautiful Lady

Petals of a thousand colours,
Caresses among the flowers,
Mixing in hearts,
Luxurious dances on flights,
With glowing lights,
From very distant dreams,
Smiles between windows,
In the edges of poppies,
Proposals with interests,
For impressing blown,
Pictured with conditions,
With flattery in the halls,
The impulse between souls,
Observing the aspects,
Eager opposite to return,
Hearing their weeping grudges,
In the breaths of origin,
Go the deserted moments,
With semblance voice in oblivion,
Finding in Disappointments,
Grey Revenge for Misery,
Kneeling in Grudges,
Miserable Strategies,
In Changing Evidence,
Don't Forget Roots,
All Beat Adventures,
Back Is Your Bliss,
From Legacies to Sorrows,
Screams Rising Outs.

Mummies

In Valley of Kings,
Among Gods and Cultures,
Under Temples of Riches,
Transmitting to Infinity,
Breaths to Lives,
On the Way to the Underworld,
By Creations of the Spirit,
In the Form of Animals,
There are paths to reunion,
For following the same origin,
Dissecting him in the natron,
Dammed to his souls,
Among ornaments for the journey,
Resurrection is coated,
Delivering his powers,
In privileges destinations,
Among rites and necklaces,
Dazzling pharaohs,
His great work rises,
Worshipping his mummies,
Ascending to the stars,
At night with their guards,
The sphinges give strength,
Protectors with their image,
When the sun was opposed,
Hopes enter,
On the journey to their way,
On return they are reincarnation,
In such divine works.

Slave Nuns

Protected abuses,
From remote times,
Discretion to the Vatican,
Save monks from strategics,
With such perverse abuses,
They are the pagans in black,
For churches without justice,
Apparently noble,
Victims fall into traps,
By trusting in the executioner,
His protected structure,
With the power of hierarchy,
For so-called gods,
Priests without prejudice,
Among saved scandals,
As an eternal city,
Under cloaks of vows,
With obligatory silences,
Chastity go on juries,
Without obeying the rules,
Priests without limits,
Subduing students,
To Religious Penances,
In Guides There Are Predators,
Using the Word,
With the Fears of Perjured,
Victims Are Trapped,
While Your Sleeping Soul,
Wait to Be Awakened.

Music

No instrument origin,
They appear resonating,
The sounds of words,
With response in movements,
Give their way with objects,
Brightening from the soul,
The moments of life,
They give us magical days,
In the cores of the image,
Of such great wisdom,
In their combined art,
With the songs of birds,
Both when the wind shakes,
Shine your calls,
With the rain leave songs,
Which keep feelings,
In The Natural Myths,
Worshipping the Gods,
With gifts of sounds,
In singing to divine,
Already born with a cry,
And a silence when saying goodbye,
Entities for centuries,
With message in remoteness,
Where harmonies are born,
Music is of the unions,
It is peace with joys.

NAPOLEON BONAPARTE

General Emperor and Soldier,
Destined for Battles,
Under a Fire It Consumes,
Wind in Revolutions,
Bathing Streets in Blood,
Monarch Bursts,
By Corrupt Systems,
In Currents Go Conflicts,
Between Exercises and Troops,
Enemies Are Defeated,
1796 Risking the Exploits,
The Ambitious Conqueror,
Proudly Towards Victories,
Exploring in Intense Light,
Times of Trade and Flames,
Between Enemy Corners,
By Territory and Riches,
Egyptian Sands Whisper,
Chains of Glories Tremble,
In the Deserts of Summits,
Challenges bring charges,
With Shadow Cavalry,
By Lurking Unions,
Code in Vengeance United,
To Extinguish Fly Rise,
Van Dictators at War,
For France Is the Force,
1815 Of the Remarkable Event Order,
His Convalescence Is the Age.

Narcissism

Between the Self and the External,
Words Are Buried,
In Invisible Thorns,
With Destructive Actions,
Distinguished Appearances,
Very Powerful Heart,
Hidden in Doubts,
To Criminal Demands,
Imposing Perfections,
Under Achievements Achieved,
Being Thirsty to Conditions,
Extending seeks flattery,
In His vain pride,
Toxic is his adventure,
Delusions in Greatness,
His senses are flooded,
In danger to the environment,
With very sad feelings,
They put blame for the causes,
Integrating opponents,
Empathies of adventures,
All excessive bond,
They catch in themselves,
Solitude with distance,
Being foolish without harm,
It is only left in their exploits,
To the forgiveness of instincts,
The love that surrounds us,
It is reciprocal of it.

NATIVES

Ancestors from ancient,
Ancient branches on,
From the divine mothers,
Steps of centuries Collect,
Transporting in seeds,
Roots of the vivid,
They travel flight brought,
Sharing in El Paso,
Teaching In Joys,
By which their roots,
They let go of the reprisals,
Energies were filled,
With the joys of the songs,
Feeling the connections,
Universe mind and life,
In their flames emerged,
They flooded ceremonies,
By which their peace felt,
Native communication,
Dance songs were created,
Thanking life,
That by the face was created,
They glowed entrails,
In souls they looked,
With the glitters shed,
Union of heaven and earth,
Renewing the entrances,
By harmony to life.

STREET KIDS

Between light and the dark,
Hiding cry silences,
Soils feel cold feet,
From childish steps,
Breezes carry fears,
Wandering corners tremble,
By broken hearts,
Pass dreams by slits,
No food sigh,
Numbing additions,
With pain in the wounds,
Drops fall between nails,
Stab wounds in oblivion,
Stagnant sufferings,
As in medieval times,
Dungeons as in trenches,
No weapons for fighting,
Discriminating stocks,
They chase harassed souls,
Continents between curtains,
They ride blindly,
The powers for their causes,
No sorrows break Colours,
For inequality in laws,
It is battle without honours,
No changes in currents,
Remotes in jumps,
Blind and vicious Deaf,
Murderers without justice.

THE NÚCLEI

Expansion theory,
In curious varieties,
Immersion of geometries,
In the cores their systems,
With beginnings in densities,
They are seed encounters,
They confirm stocks,
In composition of chemistry,
With fractions of elements,
Between phenomena cycles,
Everything is part of the universe,
With neutron stars,
They form bases of energies,
Every element of matter,
It is source of envelope,
For explosions of life,
From the centre information,
From the code so admirable (DNA),
For gene instruction,
Coming in vitamins,
They give functions integrating,
The membrane of the nuclei,
Connexion is pores,
Through regulations,
Metabolism growing,
With informative substance,
It goes including the process,
To the circle of life.

Autumn

Farewell of flowers,
Embracing their colours,
Picking up the sown,
The matrix for rest,
Leaving in every breath,
The seed of the past,
Covering the landscapes,
In dark beautiful shadows,
Hemispheric which hugs,
To his new companion,
Which by round in the corner,
It covers you from its snows,
When you leave the green forests,
By being reborn on your return,
Blowing from the deep,
Climbing in your streams,
Fortresses to rest,
You will return between your times,
Remind you of your songs,
With the blows in drifts,
His land is prepared,
For the bosom of his brother,
Vuelta put his sown,
Thinking between mysteries,
Where is the farewell,
He is not finished.

Pigeon

Opening the window,
It approaches flying,
A feather that took on,
glow of a glance,
Smiling and flown,
I was flying to my window,
Wrapping in his message,
Enlightened Resonance,
With colours of life,
Wordless music,
Enveloping excited,
A gentle harmony,
With the air of the breeze,
The pen gave us,
A message of life,
Teaching without words.
Energies flying,
Bringing the resonances,
Leading your way,
The union in the bowels,
Walking without borders,
The union of our souls.

Pandemics

Horror and tragedies,
It approaches by banks,
Without appreciating its currents,
They give their jumps in alarms,
Continental plague in minds,
Without prejudice to their actions,
They are ravaging villages,
By not governing the times well,
They integrate by being foolish,
Vague from navigators,
The silent epidemic,
Hidden and sweeping,
Vagabond is his world,
To the call of his sorrows,
In his painful advance,
He makes changes in lives,
Fears are his strategy,
To human with deviations,
Unfortunately time,
He only puts his measurements,
Learning in fate,
The career of the system,
The governments of powers,
Trapping with lies,
Under sorrows in its centuries,
The sighs are repeated,
Biology in the race,
It is economic control.

The Piano

Bridge notes in steps,
Speaking in a thousand languages,
Leaving time behind,
Surrounding dazzling,
Corners of forests,
Handing through halls,
Resonances that inspire,
Liberation with your notes,
Ties of lives,
Among intense fantasies,
Captivating with his strings,
To the touches of the hammer,
Energies leaves,
Healers of his spirit,
Companion on his strings,
Divine Intertwined,
Internal are his vowels,
With his positive signs,
Glow leave their traces,
Among conceived applause,
Admirable courtesies,
Colours with great flashes,
When joining among your notes,
Creations are conceived,
With enchanted messages,
Which in dreams catch us,
In the dance of life.

PYRAMIDS

A corner of wonders,
On the banks of the Nile,
Temples carry dynasties,
Between orbits of stars,
With creation to other lives,
From remote tombs,
In their souls are united,
Connections clothed,
With magnificent Pharaohs,
In image of animals,
Worshipping their gods,
Lifting in infinity,
In joys their sown,,
Handing over to plants,
Where they find beauty,
Like the air they breathe,
Hearts without greed,
To the contact of humans,
Sharing between nations,
His crops with measures,
Learning in courtesies,
Parallel reconquests,
From scriptures in the signs,
With engravings of secrets,
From highs of the summits,
The mystery of the stones,
They are the face of the universe.

The Pirates

Hunters for Realms,
Intrepid Adventurers,
In Captivated Experiences,
Leave Very Diverse Footprints,
In Ancient Generations,
With Their Navigating Traits,
A Bandit to Property,
Senseless to Sorrows,
Impose Powerful Laws,
Always Seek Rewards,
Low Acclaimed Audacity,
With their seal of origin,
They are perceived in blown up,
His expansive conquests,
By illegal shops,
Strategies go with charges,
Raise the weight of forces,
For serving their reigns,
In the search for greatness,
While emptying the peoples,
For extreme poverty,
Subduing cultures,
Claiming needs,
Entering worlds separating,
God and the devil in delusions,
By the vices of the human,
They are impregnated without words,
In silences other beings,
They live their sorrows.

Politics

Art of Negotiators,
Reconciling Interests,
Systems Between Nations,
Wandering in the Anarchist,
Group Associations,
In the Shadows of Words.
When seeing roots being born,
Rise as wise,
Without stopping the answers,
Even if time prevents you,
They do not perceive the pains,
What silence leaves traces,
In their invisible steps,
Complementing the bitter,
In their work goes a puzzle,
Overcome with strategies,
Power to riches,
Vanity is the frontier,
Sleepwalker for chasms,
With citizens asleep,
With no understanding,
Wise Forces raise commands,
In positions with respect,
They hold the origin,
For peace of the stable,
Possession in firm struggles,
With risks without prejudice,
They go the keys to failure,
By secrets that oppress.

Spring

Freshness with great wait,
Opening its doors arrives,
Giving way between its rays,
Collected in seeds,
Scattered from dreams,
Pollinating to life,
Wonders are raised,
Welcoming with their breezes,
Return to roses,
Which captivate with aromas,
In their preservative image,
The bowels of the earth,
Frolicking between roots,
The beings that wintered,
Food under the mantle,
Offering in energies,
By the circle of life,
It repairs scars,
Joys go in leaps,
Between large and small,
Observing their environments,
Of divine creation,
With their warm moments,
They awaken the paths,
Drawing with their features,
Colours to the beautiful.

World War I

Between a vague swirl,
With colourful uniforms,
In meaningless conflicts,
Under the order of instructions,
Empires go ambitious,
Clashes with sables,
Under glories so monstrous,
They do not cross except commands,
By schemes without measures,
Without waiting for traps,
Under shameful glories,
Merciless to his sighs,
The nobility crawls,
Youth to the fields,
The brave boys,
In the trenches of fear,
For honour of honour, la
Under pits of disasters,
Among such sad tensions,
Gallipoli is a beginning,
To the terrible disasters,
Between pouring so bloody,
Sommerland with cold terror,
Between gases and machine guns,
Words are fired,
In the abstract ill-formed,
Armies are attack,,
Under the mud in battles,
No exits to be free.

The Kingdoms

In powerful battles,
Trained for Empires,
Conquered Continents,
For giving kingdom to sultans,
Knights of splendour,
Under cults of warriors,
To the origin of the brave,
For calm without prophet,
Magna Carta is impregnated,
Kings of worship are created,
In very luxurious halls,
Castles in dungeons,
Hide cruel tortures,
shrewd etiquette eyes,
They are crossed with history,
It finds powers,
By civilising the faithful,
Educational brilliance,
Trained for kings,
They are integrated into palace,
By reigns nations,
Discovering characters,
From heels to the court,
The world of monarchs is born,
He worships the divine,
He who forgets the origin,
Eyes leave etiquette,
From the magnificent or terrible,
The palace is the answer.

RELIGIONS

Revelations of cults,
Catch sleeping minds,
Typical are their lies,
To climb on tops,
Connected words,
Enslave for lives,
foolish peoples without an order,
Withdrawing their forces,
No power to thought,
Blind eyes dressed them,
No colour or armaments,
Their goal was to tie them up,
With ears of an idea,
without listening to other bases,
Holding them speechless,
Among only a few words,
Obligations imposed,
As tales for adults,
The visionaries of cults,
Implanting with measures,
For suffering peoples,
Of pain and hard efforts,
Becoming beggars,
Which serve the system,
Creating him in obedience,
Fears of punishment,
These are religions,
Implementation for life.

Watches

Pioneers of the Eras,
Sense of Times,
In Lantern Glooms,
Among Irreversible Shadows,
The Sequence Gives Events,
Under Seas Sun and Moon,
Space is an Event,
From past and present,
The future gives banquets,
From lunar orbits,
Spheres in jumps arrive,
Where pendulous require,
Precision in masteries,
From ascents and descents,
Hearts of oceania's,
Of elegance and simplicity,
In Handles go intrigues,
Doors open the stages,
From stones and needles,
Cleopatra was called,
In the calculations of days,
Keys are supplied,
In whispers of bells,
The so-called are re-eded,
Between centuries the advances,
Create image events,
The story in realities,
Time is only what marks,
The clock and not life.

ROBIN HOOD

Sherwood County Nottingham,
Such a sublime archer,
Among enchanted forests,
Image of glory and feats,
Man who robs rich and tyrants,
to help humble and poor,
In the Middle Ages an altruist,
John without land under powers,
Villagers pay prices,
To unjust royalties,
Lady Marián as dreams,
It is wonder of loves,
What romance is born in pearls,
As flowing the flowing freshness,
Among joyful feats of challenges,
With her cunning between arrows,
He reigned good in his mind,
From forests with reflections,
His image was victory,
For the people in miseries,
Strengthening in minds,
The Joys that are extinguished,
They are heard in soft songs,
In the streets dances are born,
All sweetness opens,
When Robin gives his steps,
Popular his voice is impregnated,
For stories of stories,
With respect for his homeland.

Heading to Mars

From Nasa a Dream,
A Mission and a Destiny,
From an Odyssey in Bravery,
Your Career Is the Beginning,
Arrival a Challenge,
Crewed Among Unknowns,
From Orion Goes The Advance,
Experience in Sacrifices,
On Scales to Great Changes,
With spatial hazards,
It made the planet dead,
In barren air glaciers,
Under ruthless climates,
With solar radiations,
In Dynamic Storms,
Goes the Force of mind,
Exploring an Eternal World,
What Fiction of a Prototype,
Life on Mars was rising,
In Risks and Challenges,
The Expedition So Complex,
They Are Colonies of Yesteryear,
By Pioneering Martians,
In Lined Transitions,
Adventures on Return,
With Keys of the Explored,
Between Success and Risks,
Apollo Tube Your Advance,
Great time travellers.

Runes

Alphabet is your story,
Under thrones with your kingdoms,
Between peoples with your gods,
Rituals were reborn,
In the Flow of the Eternal,
Odin shaman of Nine Worlds,
The Traveler with His Charges,
Fight in Steps with Rubber,
Seek Love of the Stages,
In Visions with Alerts,
Towards night and day,
Opening to balance,
Between past and present,
The future follows the rhythm,
Between searches and desires,
Give power to teachers,
Who find under worlds,
Triggering wounds,
The aspects between spears,
They are secrets of suffered,
The terrible in challenges,
In the runes are guessed,
With Expiration to Changes,
Of Understood Failures,
In Hail Obstacles,
Give Overcome the Afflicted,
Power is in the sign,
Who marks it when deciphering it,
He makes his fate wise.

Sahara Desert

Tropical alignments,
Under sand rocks,
With hidden flashes,
Springs of hope,
With its scorching image,
Between lakes and oasis,
It is the life of a fountain,
sea without waters with storms,
From Atlantic to the Red Sea,
Its volcano so turbulent,
Offering its lagoons,
In source fountain appear,
With exuberant dunes,
Give image of other worlds,
Among such robust changes,
Of nights and days,
Under their lunar nights,
The stars go together,
In the image of whims,
Wonders are lit,
Between winds with colours,
Under channels of fresh waters,
Its roots are impregnated,
From mysterious crops,
With small living beings,
Mazes of landscapes,
Go together in the immense,
Camels highlight you,
With their image of beauty,
In the desert of secrets.

Heal Your Life

The father is universe,
Mother the earth floor,
The interiors are eternal,
Which are softened to time,
The connection is in the one,
Between the sun the clouds rise,
For hidden games,
Moon nights arrive,
Other united stars,
Awaken flames of lives,
The ashes are present,
There is no way out of oblivion,
We are all of the origin,
As children of the earth,
No limits or measures,
Strength is nature,
By which we are born,
Without it need of man,
In the energy of life,
What the source is joy,
No ideas that activate,
Vengeful thoughts,
Disguise is human,
By forgetting the divine,
Twisting in knotty beliefs,
You can extinguish your destiny,
Cultivate mutual affection,
It is healing of the way,
No borders to harm.

WORLD WAR II

Without Moral or Tolerance,
The Holocaust for Racism,
With Hostages and Obedience,
To the Power of Territories,
Armies of Honers,
From the Sky Sea and Earth,
To the Horror of Narcissism,
With Humiliating Strategies,
Lightning Plan Falling,
Only Churchill in Sacrifices,
Gigantic your efforts,
To honour nations,
The battle is responsible,
For facing the threat,
Under panic and sirens,
St Paul's between attack and flames,
For Unwavering Freedom,
Its symbol is of hope,
Between target lines,
Progress reborn,
With radar goes a destination,
Bending the enemy,
Assigning in Societies,
Advance by Impulses,
With Keys Goes Dominance,
From Computing Turing,
Systems by Blind Sorrows,
With Civilisation defenders,
Free Europe entails.

 Smiles Of The Heart

Petals spread in the air,
Singing go fine glitters,
There are streets recording steps,
Since childhood is impregnated,
A dream star,
With its silent instincts,
Summits always protects,
With tired and strong image,
Carries a big smile,
Hiding in feelings,
Pains that dragged him,
Early mornings shine,
At the table rich breads,
Bring memories to the soul,
For his brave mind,
Constant free hugs,
surrounding his loved ones,
With his grace in the dances,
By the landscapes of the friendship
With the voices of its features,
Great appreciations are heard,
By the way of the market,
His presence remains eternal,
Great fighter without fears,
His knew home harmony,
With his spirit he leaves traces,
He sighs with peace his roots,
Among blessings flowers,
Queen returns to paradise.

TAROT

Among The Hidden Stars,
Parallel Directions,
With Higher Levels,
In Infinite Science,
Extension is Domain,
Palm Is Written,
Heart Well Directed,
Always Acquires What You Learned,
In the Cosmos Interferes,
With the Shape of a Wave,
It Converts to Spheres,
In higher consciousnesses,
To the chord of the reflection,
That Illuminates the unconscious,
Hidden force that transforms,
The great sage into energies,
In the open kabbaels,
The answers always arrive,
Among illustrated arcane,
Numbers bring his work,
Hidden play practice,
Chronological to order,
To find the enigma,
Telepathic is its history,
After wrapped trajectories,
From remote times,
Inside is the key,
To open all the keys.

TATTOOS

Scars from soul,
They are intuitive signs,
Not knowing of their arrival,
They touch the wounds,
They are taxed for lives,
They are not sought and they find you,
They hold you in punctures,
Which you welcome as laughter,
Sharp Marks,
Carrying your artillery,
They claim you on their face,
They seek active glances,
They rejoice you in their image,
They punish you in their wrath,
they move in their calls,
Interest to be heard,
Messages come from the soul,
Entrails go in the blood,
by the forces to create them,
They are activated by being lived,
When his listeners arrive,
As he welcomes himself in his guides,
By embracing his sorrows,
They catch you with their Edges,
They soften the needles,
They send you out,
For the union of being spirit,
And peace goes their welcome.

TEMPLARS

Beliefs for freedom,
Among floors of powers,
Cultures are reincarnations,
From the wise as of the fool,
By encounters to roots,
They flow armer,
In intense great battles,
They unlace engage their prides,
In very diverse unions,
Each carries its weight,
Armours with prestiges,
Covering beautiful souls,
Free Men is the basis,
Scriptures of the times,
Remembering their ancestors,
With swords their honour,
In the strength of sown,
In instincts for their temples,
Warriors of time to order,
They seek faithful balances,
Times of strong minds,
No fears of wounds,
Highlights are his engravings,
Raised in chapels,
With statues firm stones,
For remembrance of courage,
of their courageous souls.

TIME

Tick tack sounds roads,
Destinations without perceiving them,
Encounters by only ideas,
Mark all the answers,
Wrapped between them,
They think they go so eternal,
Uncontrolled by stopping,
They catch our lives,
Tired are their roots,
We still are in them,
Needles invade us,
Days for lives take us away,
Using so much energy,
In things that empty us,
Smiles without joys,
They enter and leave in a hurry,
By the calculated time,
We end up in life,
Image that we pretend,
Blind to being in the soul,
More union is profit,
For fear losing goals,
Implanted as stamps,
Believing us companies,
To serve among naive,
stamps with names give prices,
In laps that do not derive,
So long is the race,
And it ends without living it.

TITANIC

Pride of the Occult,
On a Journey of Dreams,
Splendour so gigantic,
For famous stories,
Forces between distinctions,
When dangers lurk,
Appearances go the same,
Under iceberg of the earth,
Arraign in its history,
To open itself to consciousness,
All power very high,
Leading to response,
Great responsibilities,
They are lessons of events,
Reviving and recounting,
With rivals beliefs,
Leaves sad hopes,
Feelings leaves the ship,
By separate cultures,
With greatness in competitions,
Not found the giants,
Protection in the United,
Create bases with instincts,
To equal conditions,
Ceremonies on summits,
Rise in the breezes,
With beautiful harmonies,
Remembering the roots,
Of the love that gives life.

TRANSITION

Beautiful forces destined,
Beautiful and so divine,
Insisting on returns,
It becomes the united,
arrivals with joys,
Sad leave their departures,
No understanding at the pass,
For I do not remember the footprint,
Only delusions,
Same still without going found,
Between life and death,
Deceived ghosts,
fears create without calling them,
By opening the way to magics,
And clinging not to release them,
Voluntary Retained,
In dull spheres,
Souls fearing fate,
Enjoyment lost to the lived,
Only sound approaches,
To arrive meditating,
To recover your instincts,
Which in them is impregnated,
The union is in it.

A Legendary Soldier

With values of secrets,
Among legendary acts,
For battles they allocate,
Distortions in worship,
Among ritual greatnesses,
With symbols between traits,
Expansions of hardships,
Under colonial stigmas,
Feats face off,
Soldier in rebellions,
Resigning to the front,
They claim cowardice,
With military we despise,
Adding in the aspects,
Discrediting Signals,
A few pens of memories,
They carry times in passages,
Replenishing with plans,
Lighting in the steps,
Signs that have prices,
Representing schemes,
Of shining traps,
Comrades fear burdens,
Learning from their causes,
With feathers on return,
To the challenge of aids,
Egos calm their greatnesses,
In logic of silences,
Salvation shines.

TRAVEL THROUGH TIME

Without odour vision or touch,
Governs a system of changes,
Discovering in the impossible,
Dependencies with seconds,
Electrons in rhythms,
Uncontrollable particles,
Under the future and the eternal,
Are the tunnels on fire,
Explosives they catch,
The illusions of stars,
In constancy with the times,
Give responses of the image,
They are the lights without range,
They trap energies,
In contrasts by actions,
They give the use in vibrations,
Which does not dilate the phase,
In accelerated comprehension,
They are intrepid giants,
Low accelerated rhythms,
In remoteness the atoms,
With precisions extend,
In the driven matter,
As a mirror your image,
Cosmic strings convert,
Through the Universe,
Float infinite lines,
Between shortcuts of the cracks,
Go the shared times.

Summer

Sea Glare and Air,
Unseating Chains,
Preparing Freshwater,
Exotic Branches Shine,
Their Shining Dances,
With Aromas on Their Leaves,
Rainbow Flashes,
Illuminating Their Clouds,
Glow in Clear Rains,
Delivered to Pastures,
Preparing in Freshness,
The plain in green breezes,
Collecting its sown,
With its colourful songs,
Delivering to the seas,
His dazzling flashes,
What the beings of life,
Breathe from their harmony,
They release,
in their repressed bitter currents,
Covering in energies,
The efforts of life,
strengthening the spirit,
Back to thought,
Gives Peace to being in life,
Enjoying your smiles,
Learning in your sessions,
From union in joys.

WILLIAM SHEPHERDS

Among the Elizabethan kingdom,
Pride in Art Is Born,
Revolution of Thought,
Stamping the Universe,
With Nations Thriving,
There Is a Literary Giant,
A Great Wise in Culture,
William Shepherds with His Works,
Producing Great Changes,
Shining The Eras,
Called to Monarchs,
Surprising in Admirations,
Of human Passions,
In The Darkness of the Soul,
With the Shadows of Sinuous,
In Deep Paranoias,
By Fears and Weaknesses,
The Times That Are Past,
No Longer Threaten Present,
Time of the Danes,
His work HAMLET is Revenge,
His work KING LEAR his three daughters and false flattery,
His work MACBETH witch hunt and hatred,
At the time the war of the two roses, The Lancaster's and The Yorks,
His work RICARDO THIRD a villain and ambitious with the evil of tyrant,
His work OF OTELO jealousy as they damage,
From SHILO IN VERONA(Venice),

The work ROMEO AND JULIET Love and the Sincere,
His work THE DREAM OF A SUMMER NIGHT goblins and fairies........
Aspects of nature,
so miserably by judgements.

I'M REALISTIC

No embellishments or nuances,
A stream dragging,
Like painting in art,
A heart of expressions,
Various spheres flowing,
No hidden prejudices,
With a dreamy style,
To dress up as a party,
Colours wear my costumes,
For a dance with stars,
As I walk on seas,
I feel the breeze very cool,
It is the magic that takes me,
Among the clouds to the sky,
With smiles waiting for me,
As eagles greet,
With their cries of secrets,
Fly my image aside,
Where there are hardly any people,
Green forests shine,
To enter their footprints,
Attraction are their roots,
Sliding into the branches,
They sound singing without sorrow,
Some sigh of the soul,
Touch the doors of a bridge,
Leave a message to the wind,
Emotions that feel,
They place value of who you are.

Mysterious Cats

Four-legged and light,
Walking in fantasies,
Hidden mystery of nights,
a thousand sayings of seven lives,
Mirrors that are the keys,
Enigma eyes in history,
With their radars whiskers,
They hinder waves instincts,
Parabolic ears,
Collecting sounds,
Revered as gods,
In the time of emperors,
His snoring are therapies,
Sanction with energies,
Moving away bad vibes,
Powers of magic hide,
As therapies his image,
No stress crossing doors,
Balancing emotions,
Caring for heart and bones,
With instincts are enigmas,
No Revenge take a leap,
His Company carries sorrows,
They are felines of the story,
With their cluster of stars,
If the arrows did not exist,
For giving love when casting them,
His image would not triumph,
To climb in the bows.

140

TRAPPED

Walking in the past,
My memory has led me,
Preparing a path,
I have fallen into a destination,
Attending to the calls,
waves dragged,
with mandatory memories,
that went up without words,
They reached the ascent,
In the sky they reached,
the mermaids of the stars,
which my mind awoke,
Awakening from the past,
aloft of fate,
It appears on resonance,
the touch of a bell,
Teaching that life,
is the soul of a flame,
Lit only, to called ESPERANZA.

Printed in the United States
By Bookmasters